GREAT PHOTOGRAPHERS OF
WORLD WAR II

GREAT PHOTOGRAPHERS OF
WORLD WAR II

CHRIS BOOT

Crescent Books
New York/Avenel, New Jersey

Contents

This 1993 edition published by Crescent Books,
distributed by Outlet Book Company, Inc.
a Random House Company,
40 Engelhard Avenue,
Avenal, New Jersey 07001

Produced by
Brompton Books Corp.
15 Sherwood Place
Greenwich, CT 06830
USA

ISBN 0-517-08660-3

Printed in Italy

Page 1: An American soldier with an infant found wedged under a
rock, Saipan.
(*W. Eugene Smith*).

Pages 2-3: Australian troops advance through smoke, Western
Desert (a scene set up by the photographer and troops during a
period of inactivity).
(*Len Chetwyn*).

Left: A crew member of a Lee-Grant tank, Western Desert.
(*Cecil Beaton*).

INTRODUCTION

In the mythology of photojournalism, images of Vietnam helped change the course of war. A year after the US military photographer Ronald Haeberle documented the massacre of Vietnamese villagers by American GIs at My Lai in 1968, the pictures were published in the *Cleveland Plain Dealer*. Newspapers and magazines broke with contemporary conventions of journalistic good taste as they republished the pictures across the USA. A media deluge of violent war images had begun, assaulting the American public and feeding national debate about the price being paid for a possible victory against communism.

President Nixon later claimed that the Vietnam War 'the first in our history during which our media were more friendly to our enemies than to our allies.' A vigilant press had helped win or lose the war, depending on how one looked at it, by effectively challenging public support for the war and the will to fight; by pursuing the truth even and especially when this didn't serve America's military and strategic interests for the duration of the conflict.

It might then be assumed that the business of managing the news and controlling photographers' access to war, handled so efficiently in the Falklands (1982), at the invasion of Grenada (1983) and during the Gulf War (1991), are phenomena built on the lessons of Vietnam. But since its invention, photography and its ability to evoke reality has been used as a tool in waging war, shaping the way war is both perceived and fought. What made Vietnam different from other major twentieth century wars was that the American strategy of relying on the media to be 'on team' disintegrated. This had never happened to any major world power beforehand, and has not been allowed to make a difference since. Warring powers have now learnt how to exploit a 'free press', while controlling the making of powerful images.

The photographers of World War II were models of loyalty and never strayed 'off team.' We think of photojournalists now (or at least the best of them) as independent, self-determining witnesses, combining individuality with universal concerns that rise above plain nationalism. The roots of these characteristics can be traced to World War II, yet the striking feature of photography during this war is the extent to which all the photographers involved consistently and professionally served their national governments' war interests.

Left: PK photographer Benno Wundshammer (at right) accompanying a Luftwaffe communications unit during the battle for Stalingrad, October 1942.

Right: Hanns Hubmann (with camera), attached to the PK, pictured in the depths of the Ukrainian winter, 1942.

It's not that photographers were propagandists exactly: they weren't employed to conceive propaganda strategies or to manipulate information and were rarely their own editors. Yet whether they worked for civilian or military outfits, everything they produced was assessed and vetted for its propaganda value – even if the authorities of each nation were rarely in a single mind about what this was. General Eisenhower, the American who became the Supreme Commander of Allied Forces in Europe, was unequivocal: 'Correspondents have a job in war as essential as the military personnel . . . Fundamentally, public opinion wins wars.' The public relations business involved the production, distribution and use of rhetorical images to win hearts and minds, to promote or counter the truth depending on the circumstances, to draw attention to success and qualify or disguise failure. Central to the war effort of every nation involved, photographers were the propagandists' foot soldiers.

This was literally the case with the German war photographers who were trained and armed militia-with-cameras, employed by and subject to the military. There were no civilian war correspondents, and notions of journalistic independence did not apply. Photographers were conscripted en masse into the German propaganda divisions, the PK (*Propa-*

ganda Kompanien), whose declared aim was to influence the course of the war 'by psychological control of the mood at home, abroad, at the front and in enemy territory.'

Before America joined the war and while Britain struggled to define its information objectives, the world media relied on PK-supplied photographs for its visual reports on conflict in Poland, Norway and Finland. Germany scored notable propaganda victories early in the war. For example, photographs were distributed showing the Siegfried Line, Germany's completely inadequate Western defense, which led Americans to believe it 'magnificent.' The PK photographers exclusively recorded the fall of France and the cloak of heroism their images lent the German war effort contributed to keeping America out of combat.

The German military magazine *Signal* became Europe's best-selling magazine between 1940 and 1945, reaching a circulation of 2.5 million in 1943. Perhaps the most striking military magazine ever produced, it was developed out of the *Berliner Illustrierte Zeitung* (the magazine which, along with the *Münchner Illustrierte*, conceived the photo-essay and the human-interest story). With an acute editorial intelligence and translated into 20 languages, it was a powerful tool for promoting Germany as Europe's benefactor and protector.

Unlike propaganda produced for internal consumption it presented the British as 'noble opponents foolishly led to oppose Germany.' It didn't whip up anti-semitism, but was slickly opportunist in its racism, portraying the Americans as decadents corrupted by miscegenation and running picture stories about the French and British exploiting their 'uncivilized' colonial troops; propaganda strategies that touched raw nerves among their enemies. One 'Order of the Day' demanded: 'Where possible, all Propaganda Companies should swiftly seek an opportunity to produce pictures that show particularly well-built German soldiers confronting particularly repulsive-looking Senegalese negroes, or enemy troops of other colors. The concern is to show clear racial contrasts.'

Signal's photography was the main vehicle of its propagandist intentions. In an early issue, its editors staked the currency of the magazine on its journalistic authenticity, where stories:

'do not emanate from editorial offices or club chairs, nor are any of the illustrations taken from archives. No. All of them are a living and vivid part of the war itself from day to day. [The photographers] are not press photographers in the accepted sense of the words. They are like their comrades, soldiers of fighting units and at the same time soldier war correspondents.'

The PK, 12,000 strong at one point, lost the trust of its German audience with its wild fantasies of victory upon victory during the disastrous Russian campaign. Divisions broke out between the Propaganda Ministry and the Wehrmacht high command, and, with it, *Signal* lost its sense of purpose. It eventually re-

sorted to a mix of showbusiness and ephemera, passing off re-runs of earlier victory stories as current news, turning their initial statement of values on its head as good tidings for the German war machine ran out. The word 'defeat' was never used. Yet for years *Signal* was a seductive mix of romance, action and ideology perfectly focused in its heroically made photographs of heroic German deeds.

This photo-propaganda lead had much to do with Germany's string of early victories; it was much easier for a combat photographer to work decisively and productively with an advancing, victorious army than with losers in retreat. By any comparison Britain was ill-prepared, inexperienced and complacent. The Germans understood exactly the value of appropriately chosen and distributed photographs from the front to

project their achievements and their version of the news. The British, meanwhile, working initially on their successful World War I propaganda model, demonstrated a traditional and paternalistic distrust of the press and scant regard for the truth.

Recruitment of military photographers was reluctant and slow, and facilities for civilian correspondents negligible. There wasn't much to report during the early months of the war, but field censorship thwarted the little there was. The

Below: This photograph of the dome of St. Paul's Cathedral shrouded in smoke, taken at the height of the Blitz, is by Bert Mason of the *Daily Mail.* It powerfully evokes the spirit of an embattled England standing alone against the might of Hitler's war machine in the second half of 1940.

Royal Navy decided it had no space on its ships for correspondents at all, and British magazines had to use German photographs for lack of anything from their own authorities. In its protest against the 'club chairs' of the Ministry of Information, *Picture Post* even published blank pages, thanking the Ministry for all the photographs they were failing to supply. Joining the war in the West in 1942, the Americans brought the media customs of a more liberal society, the provision of better facilities for the press and the example of higher status offered its military photographers.

The British began to publish their own forces magazine, *Parade*, in August 1940. All archives relating to its production are lost, but the anecdotal story of its foundation is that Randolph Churchill (Winston's son sent to Cairo to act as his eyes

and ears, and put in charge of Information and Propaganda in the Middle East) saw a copy of *Signal* which arrived in Cairo via Turkey and felt the British had to compete. Although *Parade* succeeded in reaching a circulation of 100,000 throughout the British forces, it never seriously rivaled *Signal*, either in power or quality. But it was a triumph over limited resources (initiated with a budget of £100 and run on a shoestring) and its photography did enliven the army's self-image. Printed in Cairo, it took full advantage of being produced at the center of military censorship in the Middle East; by an arrangement with the censors, *Parade* editors could pick what they wanted from the stories filed by military and press photographers working in North Africa and the Mediterranean.

However, Britain rarely seemed to know where its best propaganda interests lay. As late as 1942, the already accomplished *Picture Post* photojournalist Bert Hardy experienced a saga indicating how Britain was wasting its best photographic resources. In his autobiography Hardy describes the humiliations of being conscripted into the Army and, on a six-week course, trained to take photographs by people who knew much less than he. Issued with bulky out-of-date cameras, Hardy used his own until they broke, the Army refusing to have them repaired. Hardy philosophically rationalizes the measures taken by the Army to prevent his usefulness: 'If I had been a commissioned officer, or a war correspondent, I would have had a lot more freedom. But then again, as a war correspondent entitled to use my own cameras to do my own stories, I probably would have taken more risks and I might not be here now to tell the tale.' The Americans, by comparison, in early 1941 were offering their Signal Corps photographers four months of training by professional civilians, with work experience organized by *Life*, other magazines and the news photography agencies.

Reading the 'Regulations for Press Representatives Accompanying a Force in the Field' issued by the British War Office, one might assume that the one concern of the censors was to prevent operational details reaching the enemy. Beside listing 'matters to which reference is forbidden' for military reasons (like place names, details of troop movements and camouflage methods), it placed a central condition on correspondents: 'Undeveloped negatives of photographs must be handed to a PR Officer, who will arrange for their censorship and transmission to the addressee.'

This meant in reality that PR officers had total control over the output of all press photographers, in addition to the control they exerted over where, when and how photographers reached areas of combat. Beside regard to necessary questions

Left: Bert Hardy (at left, with pistol) with three German prisoners, France 1944. Hardy, initially a photographer with *Picture Post*, was conscripted into the British Army in a similar capacity in 1942.

of military secrecy, they and the Ministry used their power freely to determine what pictures and news reached their most important audience: the British at home. Keeping the British in the dark about anything that might raise questions about the conduct of the war was a primary, if unstated, objective, and for much of first half of the war this applied to everything resembling solid information.

The news management strategies of other national governments at war were tailored to their own press traditions and methods of control. All shared the objective of amplifying good news and limiting the damage of the bad. The US government, in a society where institutional 'freedom of the press' was more developed than elsewhere, understood the role its media could play in generating and boosting domestic morale, providing the state didn't play its hand too heavily. None of the parties involved wanted to reproduce the public relations mess of World War I. Then the propaganda intention was to promote the belief that the US would triumph effortlessly and quickly without real sacrifice. This had required the faking of favorable news for the Americans, resulting ultimately in the loss of credibility of both government and press.

A few days after Japan bombed Pearl Harbor in December 1941 (the event that led decisively to the USA's declaration of war against Germany and Italy as well as Japan) Henry Luce, publisher of *Time* and *Life* magazines, wrote to President Roosevelt:

'In the days to come – far beyond strict compliance with whatever rules may be laid down for us by the necessities of war – we can think of no greater happiness than to be of service to any branch of our government and to its armed forces. For the dearest wish of all of us is to tell the story of absolute victory under your leadership.'

Whether Luce was flattering Roosevelt to preserve his own relative freedom or offering the subtlest of threats, the fact is that the *Time Life* empire worked freely and without coercion toward Roosevelt's war aims. *Life* became, in the words of one of its editors, Loudon Wainwright, 'a sort of national house organ,' articulating national aims arguably better than the government itself. Appropriate to a relationship 'far beyond strict compliance,' *Life* received preferential treatment from the US censors while, in Wainwright's words, it 'exposed embarrassing shortcomings in war production, quarreled with military tactics and grand strategy and in 1944 came out strongly for Republican Thomas Dewey' (then campaigning against Roosevelt's successor, Harry Truman).

Left: As this image taken by Hanns Hubmann indicates PK photographers were very much part of the Wehrmacht. Note the unusual 'double' Leica camera and the ubiquitous Luger pistol stuffed into the boot. The gaiters at right suggest a Red Army prisoner.

Like *Signal*, photography was central to *Life's* war-winning strategy. The connections between its ideological, propaganda and photojournalistic purposes was made explicit in a self-promotion *Life* ran in the issue of 30 November 1942:

'*Life* serves as a force in creating a sound, practical Psychological Front in the common, united effort to win this war and worldwide freedom . . . never had *Life* glossed over the horrors that stalk in the wake of the Axis aggression, but has shown war as it really is . . . stark, brutal and devastating. *Life* shows its readers in vivid picture-story form what this war *looks* like, *feels* like and *does* to people.'

While other American magazines used photographs to illustrate text, *Life* ran photographic features where the text was ancillary. It thrived on the photographic fecundity of war. 'Showing war as it is' became its anthem and manifesto, and accounted for its commercial success. It reached a circulation of six million copies a week by 1945 leading its nearest rival by 4.5 million.

This became its inspiring invitation to America's best photographers to join the endeavor, the stimulus of its new photojournalism encouraging many photographers out of the studio. Reportage had begun in Germany in parallel with technical developments: the lightweight Leica first went into production in 1924, and with another German invention, the Ermonox camera with its fast Ernostar lens, the means existed by the early thirties for spontaneous, candid photography in low-light. Gradually these transformed magazine photography everywhere with the emigration of German photographers and editors to Britain and the USA on Hitler's accession to power in 1933. It was in *Life's* editorial hands, during and after the war, that the reportage picture-story reached its peak.

Much as *Life's* declarations suggest an interest in the objective truth of war, concern with realism never superseded its self-confessed nationalist aims. Its 'realism,' however groundbreaking, was a style; although its codes and conventions were not immediately visible, it was no less a vehicle for propaganda than the styles it displaced. This can be shown in the entirely different treatment *Life* meted out to America's different enemies where photojournalistic images supported particular ideological attitudes. The Germans and Italians were Europeans, culturally integrated members of America's own white heartlands, and were hence represented with some deference. Distinctions were frequently made between the evil Nazis and the merely misguided German people. The Japanese on the other hand were viciously stereotyped, and *Life* didn't hesitate to exploit American ethnocentricity in characterizing the 'Japs' as treacherous and barbaric, inhuman and inferior. Arguably it was necessary to establish a climate of hate to sustain warfare and make it possible for American boys to kill in cold blood in the Pacific. Like other magazines *Life* was either subliminally subject to the pervasive racism of the time or it

Left: The effects of a flame-thrower on one of the Japanese defenders of the Marshall Islands, photographed for *Life* by George Strock. Unlike the dead of the European Axis powers, the Allies appeared to have had no qualms about displaying the death agonies of the Japanese.

Left: The effects of a flame-thrower on one of the Japanese defenders of the Marshall Islands, photographed for *Life* by George Strock. Unlike the dead of the European Axis powers, the Allies appeared to have had no qualms about displaying the death agonies of the Japanese.

Right: Breaking a taboo. These three Americans died during landings on Buna beach. Taken by George Strock, this controversial image was printed full-page in *Life*. The caption stated: 'dead men have died in vain if live men refuse to look at them.'

expressly pursued a policy of racial character assassination for propaganda purposes.

This uneven-handedness is reflected in the use of photographs of enemy dead. The Germans and Italians were usually accorded a respectful dignity in death, with faces rarely shown and without juxtaposed scenes of indifferent or cheerful Allied troops. No such scruples guided representation of Japanese dead. The extreme is illustrated by images run by *Life* a week before the Japanese surrender. Titled 'A Jap Burns,' six pictures used in sequence show an Allied soldier burning a Japanese commando to death with a flame-thrower, the victim shown in the various stages of his death throes, concluding with his blackened and burning corpse. German and Italian soldiers were never shown in such undignified circumstances, nor one supposes would it have been acceptable to contemplate similar Allied atrocities against them – despite the German's mighty lead over the Japanese in the war's atrocity stakes. Mutilated caucasians were simply taboo.

As for photographs of American dead, time-honored practice (at least since the Spanish-American War) determined that they should not be shown. A new Office of War Information ruling in mid-1943 followed editorials in *Life* over a period arguing that the American public should be allowed access to such images, to see more of how 'war really is.' Until then it had addressed US casualty levels pictorially by featuring studio portraits of those known to have died in battle. One of the first three images released following the new ruling was a photograph by *Life*-staffer George Strock of the bodies of three

American soldiers in the sand on Buna beach, New Guinea, published full page by *Life*. The image was from a series of photographs which had been run seven months previously showing the fight for Buna beach (not an uncommon time lag; the first revealing photographs of the bombing of Pearl Harbor weren't released until a year after the event). *Life*'s editorial accompanying the newly released photograph of the three dead Americans read:

'Last winter . . . we told about Bill, the Wisconsin boy, how he struggled through the dark and nervous jungle, stalking Japs like a cat . . . how the Japs got him . . . so that he fell down on the sand, with his legs drawn up; and how the tide came in . . . And we said then that we thought we ought to be permitted to show a picture of Bill – not just the words but the real thing. We said that if Bill had the guts to take it, then we ought to have the guts to look at it. Well this is the picture.'

Whether pressure from *Life* resulted in the new OWI ruling is not documented, but it seems likely to have played a part. *Life* used a refrain up to and over the war years – 'Dead men have died in vain if live men refuse to look at them' – with a persuasiveness difficult to ignore. The incident gives some sense of how *Life* and the US government managed their propaganda efforts cooperatively. Certainly the policy of allowing depiction of American casualties revived and sharpened American morale when at a low ebb and was welcomed by the American public. Images of American dead continued to be handled with

extreme delicacy, and photographs never featured identifiable faces. It may be that the perceived success of the change of policy in turn determined the freedom with which photographers and editors were able to address the circumstances in Vietnam 25 years later, though to the opposite military effect.

The Russians never sanctioned publication of images of their dead during the war, domestically or internationally. Images such as the 'Searching for Loved Ones' series taken by Dmitri Baltermants following the battle for Kerch in spring 1942 (where 176,000 Russians were killed retreating from the German offensive) rank among the most powerful statements of the experience of war ever made, and surely would have helped the mobilization of international opinion and resources in Russia's favor had they been released. But such was the taboo surrounding anything that might undermine the glorious heroism of the Russian soldier, especially an image of a dead one, that it is doubtful whether Baltermants in this case even presented his images to the local censor.

It was another 30 years before Czech photo-historians Daniela Mrázková and Vladimír Remeš researched and published a collection of Russian war photographs, most never

seen before, exploding any notion that the Russians had not seriously documented the war. Presumably on the grounds of necessity rather than privilege, the Russian photographers were in the rare position of processing and editing their own work, and they withheld all the images likely to offend against contemporary Russian dictat. Anxiety about simply being known to have taken images of Russian dead was such that one of the most accomplished photographers, Anatoli Garanin, allowed the Czech researchers access to his archive only with the proviso that no photographs featuring dead or dying men be published before his own death.

Indeed, the whole Russian propaganda operation functioned in a world of its own, hermetically sealed from the international dissemination of news photographs; while other governments at war, particularly the Germans and Americans, were positively wanton in their distribution of images likely to generate the most international status and sympathy, and which projected the enemy in the least favorable light, the Russians minded their own business without any apparent concern for world opinion. They denied international media access to everything of significance or value and prevented their own media from recounting what they knew. The time lag on revealing any information of consequence could be as long as five years. Kursk, probably the most important land battle of the whole of World War II and the turning point in Hitler's Russian campaign (where in July 1943 in the space of seven days the Germans lost 70,000 men, 1400 planes, 2000 tanks and 5000 other vehicles) went entirely unreported by any side. For once the Germans chose to remain silent too. The only photographs from the actual battle known to exist were taken by a PK cameraman who was captured by the Russians. Their existence only became known in the West in 1972.

While the reasons for keeping one's own people so completely in the dark about such a momentous victory are hard to fathom, the extent of Russian resistance and endurance in the face of the German invasion seem to prove that the kind of national ego-bolstering practised by the western nations simply wasn't necessary. As for the Russian attitude to their Allies' media, they had a number of grounds for suspicion. Besides US and British activity in opposition to the Communist revolution, the British also attempted to switch the war away from Germany to Russia on the latter's 1939 invasion of Finland

and, in 1941, banned the *Daily Worker*, the voice of Communism in Britain. They knew that British intelligence agencies had recruited staff among war correspondents (of *The Times* for example) and, beside, found the 'human interest' concerns of foreign correspondents trivial and ridiculous.

All photography by non-Russians was banned. In her autobiography, the *Life*-staffer Margaret Bourke-White claimed to be the only western photographer able to work inside the Soviet Union. By virtue of her ingenuity and some good contacts she managed to photograph Stalin, and she witnessed the bombing of Moscow from her hotel window. No-one else managed to by-pass the anti-camera law. The West depended for photographs of the Soviet war on rare Russian distributions, and on images by the PK and other Axis propagandists when their authorities chose to release any.

The Russian default on engagement with the international propaganda war on the terms set by its participants offers a warning against placing too much emphasis on the role of propaganda in governing the outcome of war. It is seductively easy to exaggerate the role propagandists and the tools of censorship play, not in creating approved points of view (which they do), but in determining underlying allegiances and motivations.

Left: The horrors of war portrayed by Soviet photographer Dmitri Baltermants. Entitled 'Searching for Loved Ones,' it was taken on the Kerch peninsula, the Crimea, 1942.

Right: Margaret Bourke-White, one of *Life*'s many prized contributers, pictured before an assignment with a USAF unit, 1943.

Photographers, like everyone else at war, were ideologically motivated in a much subtler way than theories of propagandist control allow, identifying with their families, neighbors and communities, regardless of the decisions of their political leaders and governments.

Sharing the experience of allied nations under fire often led photographers to make images anchored in identification with their hosts, just as they did with their own people. What photographers saw and the way they saw were shaped by broad cultural forces, rather than imposed propaganda strategies, even though these usually coincided – at least among the Western Allies. Nor were photographers passively obedient when they perceived conflict between their own experience and the censor's point of view, but this was a righteous war characterized by seamless nationalism. Photographers framed the realities they encountered accordingly.

John Steinbeck recalling experiences as a World War II correspondent in *Once There Was a War* wrote:

'We were all part of the war effort. We went along with it, and not only that, we abetted it. Gradually it became a part of us that the truth about anything was automatically secret and that to trifle with it was to interfere with the war effort . . . we wrote only a part of the war but at the time we believed, fervently believed, that it was the best thing to do. And perhaps that is why, when the war was over, novels and stories by ex-soldiers . . . proved so shocking to a public which had been carefully protected from contact with the crazy, hysterical mess.'

Steinbeck identifies exactly the balance of commitment, complicity and compromise experienced by the war's photographers too. The difference between media approaches to World War II and the Vietnam War, perhaps born out of such realizations, may be that in the latter the 'crazy, hysterical mess' became the main subject. In World War II, it was simply the interference beyond which photographers forged their despatches of national purpose.

Initially few photographers were engaged in action, but in its course World War II came to be photographed more than any war before. When the Americans first landed in Algeria (November 1942), there were just two combat photographers with the operation, but by the end of the war 500,000 still photographs had been supplied to the various American press agencies. On D-Day alone there were 100 military photographers with their units and many photographers among the 400 civilian correspondents. At the end of 1944, the Allied Press Bureau in Paris was censoring 35,000 photographs each week. The Imperial War Museum in London cares for some two million photographs by Britain's official photographers, the biggest but only one of a number of major British collections. There are no inventories of the images made by amateur photographers during the war and it is impossible to estimate the total number of images produced.

This is just the combat photography; many more photography activities had a direct application to war. Aerial reconnaissance photography, for instance, accounted for 80 to 90 percent of all Allied information about the enemy. 'A camera mounted on a P-38 has often proved to be of more value than a P-38 with guns' argued one American general involved in the mapping of more than six million square miles of enemy territory within two years. With the high altitude trimetrogon camera an area of 30 by 9 miles could be mapped in a single exposure, and photos recording long stretches of invasion beach could be made using new low-altitude, continuous strip cameras. With flashes emitting up to a billion candlepower, reconnaissance photography could be pursued at night. The images resulting from these inventions enabled an unprecedented accuracy in identifying new types of aircraft, naming enemy ships and ascertaining the extent of bomb damage.

A number of photographers now considered great worked loyally in military jobs. David 'Chim' Seymour and Norman Parkinson worked as reconnaissance photographers and readers for the US Army and the RAF respectively. Gordon Parks worked for the US Office of War Information and Bill Brandt produced an exceptional series of photographs for Britain's Ministry of Information on life in London during the Blitz – a social document made to help convince the Americans to join the war as Britain's allies, but loaded with the personal vision of an independent artist. While many photographers in enemy-held territory refused to work under occupation (Brassaï in Paris, for example), others lent their talents to the resistance effort. The French photographer Izis documented his comrades in the Resistance, keeping his codename of the period for life. Cas Oorthuys and Kryn Taconis also used their skills to serve the Resistance movement in Holland. Oorthuys produced a series of war pictures while with the 'Underground Cameramen' in Amsterdam, often hiding his camera in a coat or bag and taking pictures in secret.

Ansel Adams is not normally associated with war photography, yet he made a memorable document of Manzanar, one of the camps in which Japanese-Americans were interned between 1942 and 1944. At the invitation of a friend, the camp's liberal director Ralph Merritt, he produced the one photostory of his life, published as a book in 1944 called *Born Free and Equal*. It was so negatively received (copies were publicly burned in protest) that Adams gave the copyright and all the negatives and prints to the Library of Congress in the hope that America's shame would be objectively considered at some later point. Dorothea Lange also worked at Manzanar, as did one of the camps interns, Toyo Miyatake, a professional photographer from Los Angeles. Military orders prevented Japanese-Americans using cameras; he was allowed to compose photographs in the camp providing a caucasian tripped the shutter.

The canon of war photography might properly include a number of further activities: the production of non-documentary images for recruitment and Government advertizing; amateur volunteer schemes to document domestic life and the family for men posted away from home; portraiture, from the studio snapshots made of just about every soldier for whom the means existed to the portrayal of political and war leaders for public relations purposes (consider Karsh of Ottowa's 1941 portrait of Churchill, every nuance of the subject sharply concentrated in relation to war aims); even the idealized landscapes of home produced to help clarify what the war was being fought for might legitimately be considered war photography. Each of these activities involved countless other photographers. Because of the degree of involvement of everyone living in a country at war (at least in Europe), and because of the manufacturing and supply problems of film and chemicals leading to shortages everywhere, it is possible to relate most photographic activities of the time to one war-related application or another.

This book doesn't address the entire war photography project in these terms, but is concerned with the people conventionally considered 'war photographers': documentary still image-makers who worked in war zones making pictures to show their audience what was going on there. In this narrower, but nevertheless massive, sub-genre of photography, how do a handful of people emerge as being of special interest?

A distinction worth making here is between great photographers and great photography. The most frequently and

Right: The first (by Louis Lowery), but not the most famous, image of the flag-raising ceremony atop Iwo Jima's Mount Suribachi, February 1945. Joe Rosenthal's later shot, which caught the raising of a second, larger Stars and Stripes, is possibly the most reproduced image of World War II.

grandly reproduced image of the war, and probably the best known as a result, is Joe Rosenthal's photograph of the raising of the US flag at the summit of Mount Suribachi on Iwo Jima in 1945. In fact it was a reconstruction of the event for Rosenthal's camera; a Marine photographer Louis Lowery had been present at the actual flag raising, but the flag was inappropriately small and, more importantly, Rosenthal who was a military photographer attached to the unit had missed the important shot.

It was a moment worth capturing for the Americans, a statement that needed to be made as 7000 had died taking the tiny volcanic outcrop. American newspaper readers knew that corpses covered the beachhead for four miles and must have craved some kind of positive valediction. Every flag and every flag raising is symbolic, but this one was symbolic of more than most; the meaning of the stars and stripes had shifted subtly from war to war – from the symbol of challenge during the Spanish-American war through the badge of honor of World War I to its trenchant reference to home and the American way of life in World War II. Indicating the extent to which the meaning of the symbol was condensed and internalized by most Americans, Rosenthal recalled 40 years after taking the photograph: 'I still think of it as "our flag." That was just the way I thought about it. I still don't have any other words.'

Rosenthal's exceptional picture was seized on as an icon of the nation's glory and achievement in sacrifice. Beside its use in magazines and newspapers across the States, it was reproduced on a postage stamp, sculpted in hamburgers and ice cream and replicated as a monumental sculpture for the World War II memorial at Washington's Arlington Cemetery. It was even re-enacted in a John Wayne film as its cathartic moment with every detail of the photograph painstakingly recreated. (Three of the six men who had posed for Rosenthal were killed in the next week's fighting, but one who survived, Ira Hayes, became a national monument himself before being discredited following revelations that he wasn't at the 'original' flag raising.)

Rosenthal took the photograph as part of his day's work like any other, sending it to be developed at the standard military laboratory and forgetting about it. He had no reason to suppose he had taken a particularly important photograph. It may now be considered great by virtue of its proven relevance to America's sense of national identity, but it is the idea of the moment and the subsequent history of the image which make it remarkable. Perhaps it is unfair to single out Rosenthal as an otherwise unremarkable photographer because he made one image of abiding interest, but were it not for this image, he is unlikely to be remembered.

Another photographer whom, as it were, history chose is Yoshito Matsushige. A photographer for the Japanese daily newspaper *Chugoku Shimbun*, Matsushige was at home in Hiroshima the morning the atom bomb was dropped. 'Destruc-

tion was part of everyday life during the war so far as I was concerned,' he subsequently recalled, 'and my first instinct seemed quite normal at the time: to take some pictures.' In a daze from his own injuries, he shot the one roll of film in his possession in the streets of central Hiroshima, but because of radioactive contamination only five frames survive. They are the only photographs in existence of the apocalyptic nightmare of Hiroshima immediately after the bomb was dropped. The images are particularly valuable in that Allied military and PR efforts ensured that no professional correspondents got to Hiroshima until a month later.

Many of the images whose frequent use affirms their value as information or their power as icons of war are by photographers whose names and histories are now forgotten, or which were never linked to the image in the first place. It may be argued appropriate in the circumstances of war that when a noteworthy photograph was made, it was only its content that mattered. Where urgency or distress was involved, why should anyone be concerned with who took it? It could be considered presumptuous of photographers to wish that some kudos rub off on themselves.

There were no doubt innumerable occasions where someone with a camera happened to take a picture which was interesting or useful, one way or another, within the public domain, but where the photographer had no interest in money or glory for having taken it. Yet the opposite situation presented a constant and pressing problem for professional photographers during the war; their being accorded no recognition for being in the right place at the right time and making images of public value. There is a moral problem here which all photographers who address the suffering of others have to face, where claiming the rights of authorship appears tastelessly at odds with the circumstances. Yet the one thing that those now considered the *great* photographers of the war have in common with each other is that they managed, against the grain of most photographers' experience, fortuitously or with deliberation, to retain or later claim these rights.

Professional photography then (as now, though to a far lesser extent) bares comparison to acting: a job held to be glamorous in the public mind, but where a few celebrated stars obscure the low status of the majority in the profession. During the war this was enshrined in most of the institutions involved,

literally in the case of the British military photographers, few of whom were ranked above sergeant level. No military photographers of any nation had any rights over the photographs they made, and most of the great images stored in military museums and collections, if they are credited to an individual at all, are detailed with photographers' surnames only. Few would have been able to trace the pictures they made let alone reprint, re-present or do anything further with their work.

The pooling of correspondents' photographs was a practice established to coordinate and harness resources, prevent competition and to control the numbers and activities of photographers operating in a given area. But the terms of involvement, also the terms of access to the front in many cases, included prohibiting any reference to the photographer when pictures were despatched. The only way to by-pass the pool was to carry films out by hand, an opportunity that rarely arose.

Some photographers are 'great' in memory only, because their work is lost. Bela Zola, for instance, a Hungarian photographer born in Cairo, produced one or two stories a week for *Parade* who employed him for the duration of the war. His photographs from Sicily and southern Italy have been

Left: A front cover of the British military's wartime magazine *Parade*. An imitation of Nazi Germany's *Signal*, it helped spice up the image of the British combat forces with dramatic picture stories. Unfortunately the *Parade* archives have been lost, including most of the war pictures of Bela Zola whose cover shot is featured.

Right: Lee Miller, here pictured in Hitler's Munich apartment at the end of the war, was a fashion photographer at the outbreak of the conflict but graduated to producing war spreads for *Vogue* and US Army Public Relations.

Above: George Rodger (at right), the only British photographer to work on a freelance basis during the war, pictured during the liberation of Paris, August 1944.

described as 'among the greatest war pictures of all time,' yet all his negatives from the war years are lost along with the rest of the *Parade* archives. Even though there are the *Parade* tearsheets and a few photographs in the possession of the Imperial War Museum, Zola's reputation is unlikely to last. There simply isn't sufficient material on which to sustain his place in history.

Lee Miller is an interesting photographer to consider here. American born, she led an extraordinarily diverse life and pursued a variety of careers including model, writer and haute cuisine cook, mainly in Europe. She began the war working as a fashion photographer for *Vogue* in London. As an antidote to her regular assignments, she also photographed for *Grim Glory: Pictures of Britain under Fire*, a propaganda salvo aimed at generating support from the American public for US involvement in the war. Here she exercised her perceptive surrealist eye addressing war's assault on culture in photographs layered with meaning – her part in the surrealist art movement being her prominent claim to fame.

According to the *Life* photographer Dave Scherman, a friend who Miller later worked with closely, she was tormented by 'the threat of being left out of the biggest story of the decade' and to satisfy her appetite for engagement with war, she managed to persuade *Vogue* to procure her access to 'the forbidden areas where the excitement was.' Initially, the stories she pursued were only a short step from her fashion work, location portraiture of the Wrens (women's volunteer units) and the ATS (Auxiliary Territorial Service), for instance. Beginning to file words as well as pictures to save costs, she managed to turn a minor assignment about nurses in an evacuation hospital into a major piece of reporting which Audrey Withers, *Vogue*'s editor, described as 'the most exciting journalistic experience of the war.' She had brought war reporting to the pages of *Vogue*, and she led its development, providing five or six features a month by 1944, covering topics as varied as the liberation of Dachau concentration camp and the first fashion season of liberated Paris.

She also picked up assignments for the US Army Public Relations for whom she was working when she found herself witness to the bombing of St. Malo. The photographs she made from her hotel balcony were cause for her detention by the military – for working in a combat zone, violating the terms of her accreditation. Miller's every step forward involved breaking rules and defying convention, and her combination of guts and vision led to some memorable pictures. Yet she is less likely to be feted in the war photographers' hall of fame were it not for one particular rule she broke. Contrary to contemporary practice, she kept her own negatives and apparently failed to sign any contracts with her main client. Her son Roland Penrose found the bulk of the negatives stored and forgotten in a trunk, a discovery which began an exploration of Miller's work. Making fine prints from the best images, exhibiting them and publishing two books about Miller, her reputation was secured. *Vogue* released Penrose what negatives they had in their files in the absence of any documentation determining ownership.

If this book had been written a few years ago, before Penrose's archaeological finds and the publication of the books, Miller's work would not have featured. Even with the motivation, Penrose's enterprise was less likely to be fruitful without Miller's abandon or foresight in holding on to her negatives. Who can say how many other photographers are neglected, perhaps ones who made no single great images but whose bodies of work would sustain historic interest? Without massive research efforts it would be impossible to retrieve the work of most war photographers individually, with the majority of their pictures languishing uncataloged in military and private archives or lost altogether.

Curatorial negligence hasn't dogged the recuperation of Cecil Beaton's war work. Another photographer known for his fashion and society work, Beaton toured many of the war's combat zones, abstracting verities from the wreckage of war and documenting the parties involved. He was employed by the British Ministry of Information in 1940 to redress the short-comings of official photography at the time, perceived too 'static' and lacking 'power.' This revealed the ministry's lack of faith or interest in photojournalism; it was 1942 before official photographers were encouraged to follow the example of *Life* and *Illustrated*, and create photographic feature stories. Beaton was granted exceptional status among official photographers and worked with considerable freedom. He negotiated special terms for the handling of his work, and to this day remains the only British official whose work is categorized by his name in a special collection at the Imperial War Museum.

George Rodger was the only British photographer to work on a freelance basis during the war, a 'stringer' for *Life* magazine between 1939 and 1942 until he joined their regular staff. After his work on the Blitz, an appetite for travel and adventure was met by journeys throughout Europe, Africa and the Middle and Far East. He made powerful but restrained documents on the war, resisting the temptation of sensationalism and staking his integrity on his photographs being 'meticulously factual, honest and true – no staged effects, no Western Desert mock-ups, no falsity.'

The Western Desert, where there were long periods of military inactivity and an unchanging background, provided good opportunities for some photographers to reconstruct action for the camera. The best-known of these were made by British Sergeant Len Chetwyn and his film and photographic unit, 'Chet's Circus,' who elicited the support of troops to stage elaborate mock-ups of battle scenes. These were approved by the War Office, and although they represent an extreme of fabrication, the best of photographers often manipulated circumstances in order to make telling images. Indeed, the photographic act of forging coherent images out of chaos can be considered a form of fabrication, whether benign or calculated, with photographers manipulating meaning even when not manipulating people. It was rare then for a photographer to place his reputation on refusing to entertain any form of image construction, but Rodger's despatches, written and photographic, became trusted as reliable rumor-scotching intelligence on war in the outposts of the British Empire.

Rodger's experience as both freelancer and staff photographer during the war, with the freedoms and rights of the former significantly outweighing the benefits of the latter, fed his motivation for the founding of the Magnum photographers' cooperative, which Rodger did in 1947 along with Robert Capa, Henri Cartier-Bresson, David Seymour, Maria Eisner and Bill and Rita Vandivert. Built on the fundamental principle of photographers owning and controlling the rights to their work, albeit without the security offered by magazine employment, Magnum made its job the promotion of photographers as individuals with perspectives on the world which merited attention in their own right. Though only founded after the war, by fighting for authorship rights to photographs and in its handling and presentation of its members' archives, Magnum contributed significantly to the legacy of 'great' war photojournalism, and to the place photojournalism generally now holds in the canon of serious photographic endeavour. It opened the possibilities for independent photographic commentary on other wars and its legacy survives today throughout the photojournalism world, with many agencies now operating on similar principles and with photographers' control of their copyright a standard right rather than an exception.

Another of the few institutions which invested heavily in the identity and achievements of individual photographers was *Life*. Although it pioneered and pursued 'group journalism' for the majority of its features, it regularly credited photographers. Every week's contents page featured a box headed '*Life*'s Pictures,' often with a portrait of the photographer, either with biographical details as background to some pictures in the issue or an account of their exploits while on assignment. With this, its generous assignments and in the space it gave picture stories, it sponsored more of the legends of World War II photography than any other magazine, including Margaret Bourke-White, Carl Mydans, Andreas Feininger and George Silk. Few other magazines, even those as dependent on photography for their impact as *Life*, privileged their photographers in quite this way. *Signal*'s photographs were initially uncredited, but learning from *Life*, they began similar stories of photographers' endeavor and daring. Later, its stars like Hanns Hubmann were always credited. Even *Picture Post* after Stefan Lorant left its editorship rarely credited its photographers, nor for that matter its writers, preferring a wholly corporate personality.

It was *Picture Post* however, breaking all their conventions of anonymity, that first claimed Robert Capa 'The Greatest War Photographer in the World,' running 12 pages of pictures from the battle of the Ebro during the Spanish Civil War in its issue of 3 December 1938. Titled 'This is War' and opening with a full page portrait of Capa behind a camera, it presented the photographs as 'simply the finest pictures of front-line action ever taken.' Throughout 1938, praise had been steeped on Capa from many of America's magazines, and while the war offered the opportunity for other young photojournalists to make their reputations, the 27-year-old Capa began it with his fully intact. He remains the archetype.

He distinguished himself by consistently making his own luck, and gambling on fate became his leitmotif. His memoirs of the World War II years, *Slightly Out of Focus*, are studded with references to his gambling exploits which he used to develop comradeship with members of the unit wherever he was posted, and which in turn helped create his luck. He tells the story of how, while in London taking a seven-day break from working in North Africa, he was recalled to the USA by

Colliers magazine. With the American War Department insisting that all correspondents in Europe participate in the pool system, *Colliers* could no longer justify keeping Capa in Europe when other publications had access to his pictures and were able to publish before them.

A Hungarian by birth and traveling on some rickety papers, Capa recognized his return would result in losing his accreditation as a war correspondent. His relations with *Life* were far from healthy (he'd been fired twice and walked out on another occasion) but getting them to hire him by offering a scoop was his only hope of staying in Europe. Finding out that:

'Big things would be brewing pretty soon along the Mediterranean . . . I thought if I could get back to North Africa before the Army learned I had been fired, and if I could somehow pull a fast one and scoop the rest of the photographers, then the thing might be wangled somehow. It all seemed perfectly simple – just this side of impossible – but I had to give it a try.'

His gamble paid off. He succeeded in staying ahead of the notice of his redundancy as it pursued him to Africa (at least, he persuaded those it reached to ignore it for a few hours). Reaching Algiers he thought he was too late for a chance to witness the US invasion of Europe, but hung around the PR Office 'hoping desperately for my usual miracle.' It happened in the men's room, where he bumped into a photographer who was assigned to the invasion, had been trained over months to jump with an airborne division, but was too sick to go. Not only did Capa manage to take his place and get immediately to

the invasion airbase in the Tunisian desert, but he flew in the lead plane, photographed the 'first American to land in Sicily' before and as he jumped, processed his film back in Tunisia, made it to Tunis with the photographs and had them censored and wired to America – all before any announcement of the invasion had been made. Confronted again with orders to return to the USA, he jumped himself that night knowing it would take some time before anyone would catch up with him in Italy. Three weeks later he finally heard he had been hired by *Life*.

It turns out that a fundamental component of Capa's legendary status was his ability to cultivate it so successfully himself. *Slightly Out of Focus* was written with movie rights in mind, and contains some wild embellishment of the truth. In his (authorized) biography of Capa, Richard Whelan corrects a few points in the above story; Capa didn't have to worry about losing his access to the front – he could have been sure *Life* would hire him had he swallowed his pride and asked. The armada carrying troops to Sicily had already left when Capa arrived in Algiers and his pictures of the first men in were in fact of the 504th Parachute Regiment's 3rd Battalion, reinforcements jumping in to support the first troop wave a day after their arrival. At that point, he still had a week before losing his accreditation, and he traveled to Sicily by supply ship, rejoining the 504th a week after he'd photographed the drop.

Capa admits on the dust jacket of *Slightly Out of Focus*:

'Writing the truth being obviously so difficult, I have in the interests of it allowed myself to go sometimes slightly beyond and slightly this side of it. All events and persons in this book are accidental and have something to do with the truth.'

Indeed, fictionalizing his adventures never harmed his reputation. They may even have enhanced it, proving his ability to wring every drop of juice out of a good story. Certainly they contribute to the legend of Capa; romantic, courageous, daring and larger than life. Even his name was an invention, based on an allusion to Frank Capra and Hollywood (he was born Endre Friedmann). Knowing some of the facts that contradict his version of the invasion of Italy story only heightens our sense of his

Above: Robert Capa as photographed by George Rodger. Capa, probably the best known war photographer, followed the Allies from North Africa to northwest Europe. He lost faith in the point of war photography after Hiroshima, but resuming his conviction, he died in 1954 covering France's war against the Viet Minh.

Right: The airborne invasion of Sicily as reported by Robert Capa. Sacked by *Collier's* magazine and due to return to the USA, Capa's pictures of the first Americans into Italy were his attempt to scoop his way into *Life*'s employ and a chance to stay in Europe.

audacity. Not only was his war full of genuine scoops but, as Whelan points out, Capa was so familiar with putting himself at risk for pictures that while he adorned the narrative of his life, he consistently underplayed the dangers he faced to get his pictures. 'If your pictures are no good, you aren't close enough' became his motto and if anyone had any doubts, his legendary status was confirmed when Capa went close one last time and lost his life during a battle in Indochina in 1954.

Capa had no interest in the art of photography in orthodox terms, and the title of his war memoirs refers to the blur in many of his best-known pictures. Rather than rendering them unusable, it added a further layer of drama and heightened the sense of proximity to the action (especially true of the few frames that survived from his take at the D-Day invasion). One man who was consummately concerned with the craft of photography as part of a fully-rounded technical and conceptual practice was Edward Steichen who, like Capa, surpassed his clients' and the propaganda brief, making images which shaped the possibilities of the medium.

In fact, Steichen's role in the war was only partly as photographer. Already American documentary photography's father-figure, Steichen was hired to run what became the most exceptional Allied military photography operation of the war. This was the result of his own initiative. He approached the US Navy, whose interest in photography at the time was limited to its value in reconnaissance and training, and persuaded them that photo documentary 'in addition to serving as a simple recorder of facts and faces, could, in the right hands, serve as a powerful instrument for distilling the human meaning of complex events,' and prove 'an invaluable means to convey the human drama of the Navy's war to the American public and to future generations.' Given the opportunity, he recruited a crack team of documentary and other photographers, illustrators, printers and lab technicians, including Horace Bristol and Charles Fenno Jacobs (both ex-*Life*) Charles Kerlee (one of the West Coast's best young commercial illustrators) and Wayne Miller (then a young Navy ensign). They and others all went on to distinguish themselves under Steichen's singular and uncompromising guidance.

He was working to his own agenda. 'Bring back something that will please the brass a little bit, an aircraft carrier or somebody with all the braid,' he told his photographers. 'Spend the rest of your time photographing the man . . . the little guy, the struggle, the heartaches, the *dreams* of this guy.' As both photographer and editor, Steichen sought images of graphic power with an epic sense of spectacle. But more than these, he sought to focus attention on the men, as individuals perhaps, but more importantly as heroic symbols of America's collective experience of the war, to feed its national imagination. Steichen's success, as with the best of the German PK photographers, was rooted in an understanding of the iconographic potential of men in action and of nationalist idealism.

Steichen was an editor/photographer who created his own military brief in the first place and then transcended it, achieving a status for himself and his photographers rarely attained by others working for anyone's military and far more than a mere propagandists' foot soldier. He had established his reputation as both photographer and curator long before the war (he was 62 when he gained his Navy commission) and many of the photographs he and his unit made during the war are dramatically and technically superior to the bulk of even the best war photography. Resuming his curatorial work at the Museum of Modern Art after the war, he mounted 'The Family of Man' exhibition in 1955. Created, he says in his catalog introduction, 'in a passionate spirit of devoted love and faith in man' and with pictures demonstrating 'the essential oneness of mankind throughout the world,' this enormously popular show articulated a philosophy for post-war photojournalism. Born out of the suffering of war and in sharp opposition to growing cold war rhetoric, it rejected national for universal perspectives on man's condition.

One photographer who struggled with a complex relationship to war, and to the nation for whom he was its witness, was the American W. Eugene Smith. (Steichen tried to recruit him for his unit, but Smith was rejected on the Navy's medical criteria). He became perhaps the model of postwar concerned humanist photojournalists, beginning the war a naive and optimistic idealist and ending it hardened and in constant battle with his conscience. In his notes to the first of many lectures he gave about the war years, he wrote:

'I did not cover this war to give people a thrill . . . I wanted pictures of the emotions of war, that would reach and grasp people by the throat until the nature of war was forced into their thought channels – I wanted somehow to make those people think, and think enough until they were determined that there should be no more wars . . . I must do everything that is in my physical and mental power to add my straw to the prevention or delaying of the next war.'

This may be postwar rationalization, but it was certainly in his power to make pictures of dramatic and troubling intensity; photographs carefully crafted both in the heat of action and in the darkroom which were more than products of chance and ambition, and which anticipate the work of later anti-war photographers.

Seriously injured at Okinawa, Smith didn't photograph for a year, until he made perhaps his best known picture 'The Walk to Paradise Garden,' featuring his two children walking out of a dark bower in the woods into a light clearing. Smith spoke later of planning the image for three weeks, and talked of it being a 'printable reproduction of a mental realization.' Although some of Smith's war pictures are raw in their power, many are as considered as 'Paradise Garden,' 'mental realisations' of the hell and injustice of war, as if the conscience of art could do

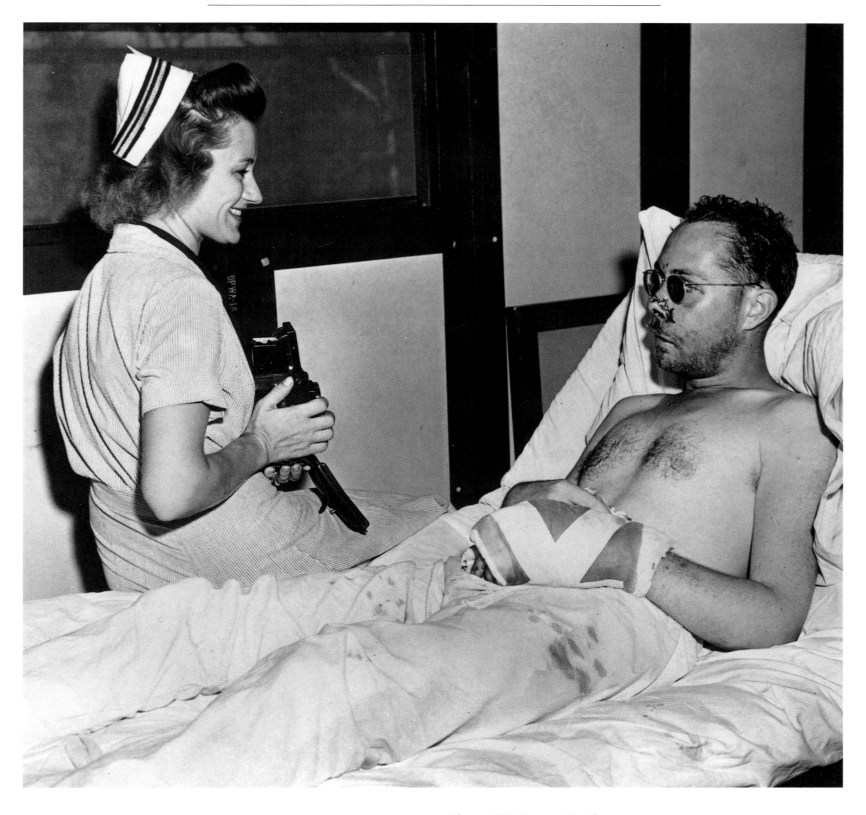

battle with war itself.

Images by a number of the Russian war photographers match Smith's for their drama, emotion and operatic scope, and while they are directly concerned with the Russian experience of the war rather than anyone else's, seem to stem similarly from humanist as much as nationalist concerns. The notable Russians include the committed social reporter Georgij Zelma, best known for his pictures of guerrilla warfare during the siege of Stalingrad; the TASS photographer Max Alpert, whose photograph of a battalion commander with pistol raised and in full cry became a symbol of the victorious advance of the Soviet Army into Western Europe; Dmitri Baltermants, a die-hard pacifist who worked for the Red Army and *Izvestia*, and

Above: W. Eugene Smith recovering from the wounds inflicted by a Japanese mortar round during the battle for Okinawa, May 1945. Smith became renowned for his troubled, disturbing accounts of the horrors of conflict.

Mikhail Trakhman, a Red Army correspondent, both of whom made persuasive indictments of war in cinematic tableaux.

Another Russian, Anatoli Garanin who photographed on the front throughout the war for *Frontovaya Illustracia*, has accounted for the humanistic ethic guiding his work in terms of his christian faith. This gives some indication of the gulf between the Russian photographers' official brief and their actual concerns, illicitly anticipating the later humanism of western photographers. Perhaps it was that the scale and hellishness of war on Europe's Eastern Front was especially and horribly photogenic compared with other theaters. Certainly some of the great Russians made few images of lasting interest either before or after the war – as if the beginning of war released the spontaneous lament of the 'Russian Soul,' with photographers reverting to familiar, patriotic obedience following victory. Whatever the motives, the five Russians named here rank alongside Steichen, Capa and Smith as perhaps the greatest figures in the photography of the war.

But what does a war photograph tell us about war? Photography may seem to be about information, satisfying a need to know the facts, but while its military applications testify to its functional value, most war pictures reveal very little descriptive data and rarely show a significant event taking place. They convey a sense of what war is *like* by concentrating on the details; the expression that crosses a face, a tiny moment in the action, a mark of death. Often the smaller the detail, the greater the expressive power of the image. While some of the most powerful images of war work like martial paintings of earlier centuries, stirring calls to the valiant, perhaps the best are more like *haiku* verse: approaches to the vast meaning of the whole via the smallest fragments of the particular. If they really work well, they are proportional to the facts of war: the intense poignancy of a mother's grief on the Eastern Front in relation to the other millions of Russians who shared her son's fate.

There's a moral problem at the heart of war photography. Part of its awful appeal is its ability to combine terror and beauty in equal measure. As Eugene Smith said:

'Sensually, there is something magnificent and beautiful in war – the slow jogging of these damp, helmeted men against the eerie light of flares, the silhouette of smashed buildings, the flame-throwing tanks with a burst of spectrum, the sight of planes falling before patterns of long tracers, the twinkling of anti-aircraft fire – these are magnificent sights until you think.'

Left: TASS photographer Max Alpert's image of a youthful Red Army officer leading his command into an attack dramatized the Soviet Union's victorious advance against the Wehrmacht.

Above: The battle for Kerch, 1942, by Anatoli Garanin, where 176,000 Russians were killed retreating from the German offensive.

Even when the sights aren't magnificent, the photographer's job is to lend them grace, in composition and balance. Some found the terror and beauty irresistible, even addictive. The audience too is complicit in its proxy voyeurism. By looking, we satisfy not our desire to understand the facts, but our need to face a little of our own fear and mortality. Albeit in the comfort of our homes.

World War II happened at a threshold for the possibilities of photography, intimately bound into developing humanist aspirations for universal peace among the 'family of man.' But foreseen in its beginnings was its end. Robert Capa felt that after Hiroshima (he spoke before full knowledge of the horrors of Auschwitz) there was no further point to war photography. If the dream wasn't over then, it must be now. The impulse to address war in images, to articulate experience and share feeling, may be just as strong and valid as ever, but war photographers have had to give up hopes of stopping war. Humanity might be in a worse mess without the testimony of the photographic witness; images may even have helped curtail the Vietnam War. Yet there has never been a day of peace since 1945. The world lurches toward the millenium wrought by wars and rumors of more, without big dreams to give us hope. All we can do is look.

An East London Underground station, November 1940.
(*Bill Brandt*).

Left: Civilian casualties of a Luftwaffe bombing raid, London, the Blitz.
(*George Rodger*).

Above: Journalists waiting for the 'imminent' German invasion, England, August 1940.
(*George Rodger*).

FUSELAGE & RESERVE FUEL

Above: An American pilot flying with the Royal Air Force, England, 1941.
(*Robert Capa*).

Right: A welder at work in a British shipyard.
(*Cecil Beaton*).

Overleaf: Crew members of *U-96* at work during an attack by a British escort vessel.
(*Lothar-Günther Buchheim*).

Above: The shattered remains of a German tank in the Western Desert, North Africa.
(*Cecil Beaton*).

Right: The grave of an RAF officer buried by the Afrika Korps, North Africa, 1941.
(*George Rodger*).

Hier ruht
ein unbekannter engl. Leutnant
im Luftkampf gefallen
am
14. 6. 1941

Soviet anti-aircraft fire lights up the night sky, Moscow, 1941.
(*Margaret Bourke-White*).

Soviet infantry attack on the Smolensk front.
(Dmitri Baltermants).

Left: Prime Minister Winston Churchill, 1941.
(Karsh of Ottawa).

Above: Members of the American Volunteer Group, the famous 'Flying Tigers,' Burma.
(George Rodger).

Left: The aftermath of a Nazi attack in Russia, 1941. (*Anatoli Garanin*).

Above: A defender of Stalingrad, 1942. (*Georgi Zelma*).

'The irrepressible British Tommy,' North Africa, 1942.
(*Len Chetwyn*).

Left: A Japanese soldier's head displayed on a burnt-out tank, Guadalcanal, 1943.
(*Ralph Morse*).

Above: Members of the US 1st Ranger Battalion set out on patrol, North Africa, 1943.
(*Robert Capa*).

Left: German helmets collected by US troops, North Africa, 1943.
(*Eliot Elisofon*).

Above: A Papuan aiding a wounded Australian, New Guinea, 1943.
(*George Silk*).

Left: Wehrmacht assault guns on the move in the Caucasus. (*Hilmar Pabel*).

Above: The aftermath of an Allied air raid on Dusseldorf, June 1943. (*Hanns Hubmann*).

US Infantry advance through the ruins
of Troina, Sicily, 1943.
(Robert Capa).

A Sicillian policeman dispenses refreshment, Sicily, 1943.
(Robert Capa).

Italian mothers grieve for partisans killed by the Germans in the
battle for Naples, October 1943.
(Robert Capa).

Above: Working on the turret of a US bomber, Baltimore, 1943.
(*Charles Fenno Jacobs*).

Right: A flight of Grumman Avenger torpedo-bombers, Fort Lauderdale, 1943.
(*Charles Fenno Jacobs*).

Russian civilians greets one of their saviors,
Sebastopol, May 1944.
(Ye Haldei).

The ruins of Cassino, Italy, 1944.
(*Carl Mydans*).

Above: The landings on Omaha Beach, D-Day, 6 June 1944. (*Robert Capa*).

Overleaf: The cost of the D-Day landings. (*Robert Capa*).

Left: Frisking an SS prisoner shortly after D-Day. (*Robert Capa*).

Above: A Grumman Hellcat takes off from the USS *Lexington*. (*Edward Steichen*).

Advancing under fire toward Cherbourg, June 1944.
(*Robert Capa*).

Shells exploding on the island citadel of St. Malo, Britanny,
France, 1944.
(Lee Miller).

Above: French civilians and Resistance members under German
sniper fire, Paris, August 1944.
(Bert Hardy).

Overleaf: Dealing with a collaborator, Paris, August 1944.
(Robert Capa).

Fitting a new plaster cast.
(*Ralph Morse*).

Hitler, Göring and staff pictured during the Ardennes offensive,
1944.
(*Heinrich Hoffman*).

US troops advancing in open order near Bastogne, Ardennes, winter 1944-45.
(*Robert Capa*).

Above: German prisoners bring in the body of a dead GI,
Ardennes, winter 1944-45.
(George Silk).

Right: Allied troops advance into Alsace, winter 1944-45.
(Lee Miller).

German prisoners escorted by British troops, winter 1944-45.
(*Bert Hardy*).

Routine maintenance duties onboard the USS *Lexington*.
(*Edward Steichen*).

Above: After an Allied bombing raid, Berlin, February 1945.
(A. Grimm).

Right: Raising the US flag on Iwo Jima's Mount Suribachi,
February 1945.
(Joe Rosenthal).

Marines destroying a cave connected to a Japanese blockhouse,
Iwo Jima, 1945.
(*W. Eugene Smith*).

A civilian casualty of the fight for Manila, Philippines, 1945.
(*Carl Mydans*).

General MacArthur's famous return to the Philippines, 1945.
(*Carl Mydans*).

Hitler Youth members advance to engage the Red Army, March
1945.
(*Benno Wundshammer*).

US paratroopers prepare for the Rhine crossing, 1945.
(*Robert Capa*).

Left: A medic attends to a wounded paratrooper, Rhine crossing, 1945.
(Robert Capa).

Above: US troops in action, Leipzig, April 1945.
(Robert Capa).

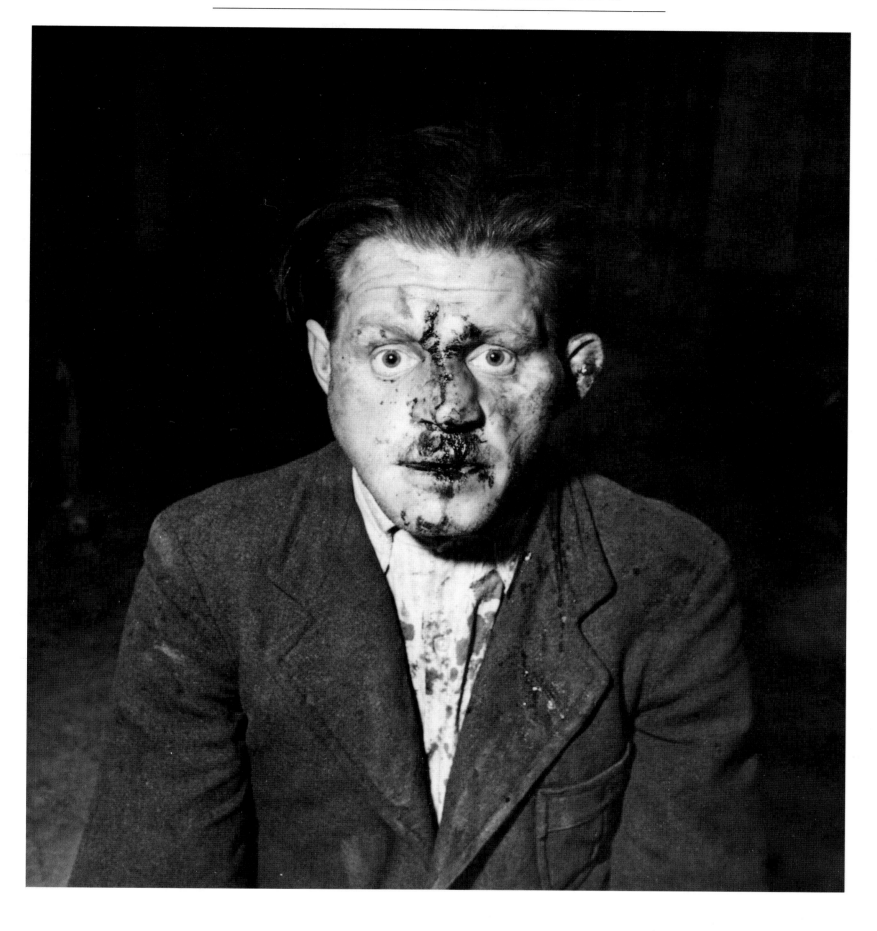

Left: The death of an American soldier, Germany, 1945.
(Robert Capa).

Above: A beaten-up guard (disguised as a prisoner) at
Buchenwald concentration camp, 1945.
(Lee Miller).

'Living dead at Buchenwald,' April 1945.
(*Margaret Bourke-White*).

The suicide of a minor Nazi official and his family, Leipzig, April
1945.
(*Margaret Bourke-White*).

PARTEIKLEIDER

German dead on the streets of Vienna, 1945.
(Ye Haldei).

Soviet troops at Torgau, Germany, May 1945.
(*Lee Miller*).

The ruins of Nuremberg, May 1945.
(Margaret Bourke-White).

The remains of a chemical plant, Ludwigshafen, 1945.
(*Lee Miller*).

The Hofbrauhaus, Munich, 1945.
(Lee Miller).

Storming the Reichstag, Berlin, May 1945.
(*Yakov Ryumkin*)

Right: 'The Banner of Victory over Berlin,' May 1945.
(*Victor Grebnev*).

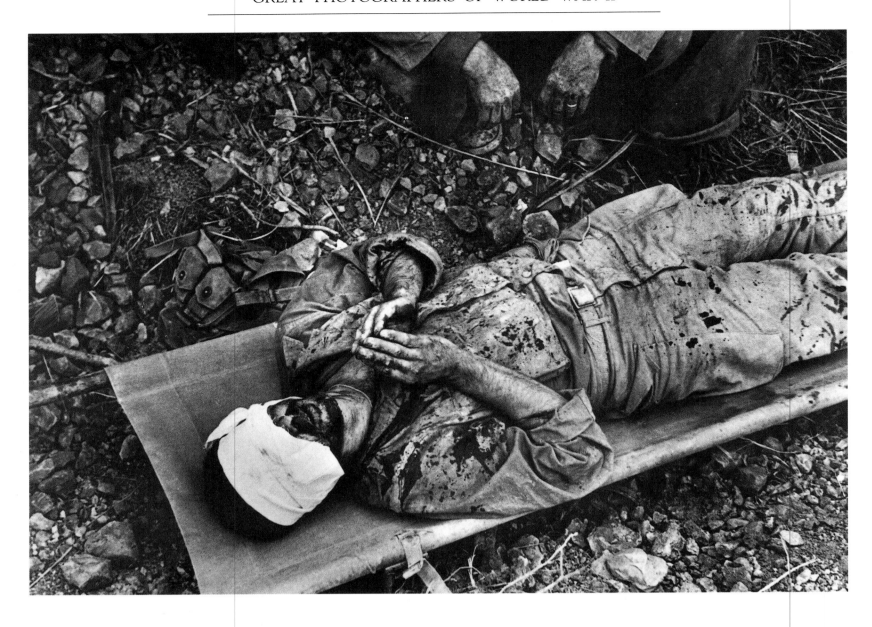

A wounded soldier on Okinawa, 1945.
(*W. Eugene Smith*).

Above: Recently liberated US civilian prisoners of the Japanese, 1945.
(Carl Mydans).

Overleaf: The Japanese surrender ceremony onboard the USS *Missouri*, 1945.
(Carl Mydans).

A victim of the nuclear attack on Hiroshima, 1945.
(*Wayne Miller*).

Tending a child of Hiroshima, 1945.
(*Wayne Miller*).

Left: Celebrating VJ-Day, Times Square, New York, August 1945.
(Alfred Eisenstaedt).

Above: The homecoming of German prisoners, Vienna, 1947.
(Ernst Haas).

Selected Bibliography

Armor & Wright, with photographs by Ansel Adams. *Manzanar*. Vintage, New York 1989.
Beaton, Cecil. *War Photographs, 1939-45*. Imperial War Museum, London 1981.
Bourke-White, Margaret. *Shooting the Russian War*. Simon & Schuster, New York 1942.
Capa, Robert. *Images of War*. Grossman Publishers, New York 1964.
Capa, Robert. *Slightly Out of Focus*. Holt, New York 1947.
Fabian & Adam. *Images of War*. Stern, Hamburg, 1985.
Graves, Eleanor, ed. *Life Goes to War: A Picture History of World War II*. Little Brown & Co., Boston 1977.
Hopkinson, Tom, ed. *Picture Post 1938-50*. Penguin, London 1970.
Hughes, Jim. *W. Eugene Smith, Shadow and Substance*. McGraw Hill, New York 1989.
Knightley, Philip. *The First Casualty*. Andre Deutsch, London 1975.

Lewinski, Jorge. *The Camera at War, War Photography from 1848 to the Present Day*. W H Allen & Co, London 1978.
Mayer, S. L., ed. *Signal – Hitler's Wartime Picture Magazine*. Prentice-Hall, London 1976.
Moeller, Susan. *Shooting War*. Basic Books, New York 1989.
Mrazkova, Daniela & Remes, Vladimir. *The Russian War 1941-45*. Cape, London 1978.
Mydans, Carl. *More than Meets the Eye*. Harper & Bros., New York 1959.
Penrose, Anthony. *The Lives of Lee Miller*. Thames & Hudson, London 1985.
Phillips, Christopher. *Steichen at War*. Harry N. Abrams, New York 1981.
Rodger, George. *Red Moon Rising*. Cresset Press, London 1943.
Taylor, John. *War Photography, Realism in the British Press*, Routledge, London 1991.
Whelan, Richard. *Capa: A Biography*. Knopf, New York 1985.

ACKNOWLEDGMENTS

The publisher would like to thank Rita Longabucco and Suzanne O'Farrell for the picture research on this title, and Adrian Hodgkins for his design work. Special thanks are due to Rolf Steinberg for his research work in Germany. The author would like to thank all those who offered their help and support during research for the text, and owes a particular debt of gratitude to Val Williams, John Taylor, Daniela Mrázková, John Easterby and George & Jinx Rodger. The following agencies and individuals provided photographic material:

Bildarchiv Preusserischer Kulturbesitz, pages: 6(Benno Wundshammer), 7(Hanns Hubmann), 12(Hanns Hubmann), 52(Hilmar Pabel), 53(Hanns Hubmann), 82(Arthur Grimm), 88(Benno Wundshammer).
Lothar-Günther Buchheim, pages: 36-37.
Camera Press, London, page: 42(Karsh of Ottawa).
George Eastman House, pages: 58(Charles Fenno Jacobs), 67(gift of Edward Steichen by direction of Joanna T. Steichen), 81(gift of Edward Steichen by direction of Joanna T. Steichen).
Imperial War Museum, London, pages 2-3(Len Chetwyn), 4-5(Cecil Beaton), 8-9(copyright *Daily Mail*/Bert Mason), 10-11(Bert Hardy), 30-31(Bill Brandt), 35(Cecil Beaton), 38(Cecil Beaton), 46-47(Len Chetwyn), 71(Bert Hardy), 80(Bert Hardy), 83(Joe Rosenthal).
David King Collection, pages: 29(Anatoli Garanin), 102(Yakov Ryumkin), 103 (Anatoli Garanin).

© Life Magazine/Time Inc., pages: 1(W. Eugene Smith), 14(George Strock), 15(George Strock), 32(George Rodger), 40(Margaret Bourke-White), 48(Ralph Morse), 50(Eliot Elisofon), 51(George Silk), 62(Carl Mydans), 74(Ralph Morse), 75(Heinrich Hoffman), 78(George Silk), 84(W. Eugene Smith), 85(Carl Mydans), 86-87(Carl Mydans), 94(Margaret Bourke-White), 99(Margaret Bourke-White), 104(W. Eugene Smith), 105(Carl Mydans), 106-107(Carl Mydans), 110(Alfred Eisenstaedt).
Magnum Photos, pages: 22(George Rodger), 24(George Rodger), 25(Robert Capa), 33(George Rodger), 34(Robert Capa), 39(George Rodger), 41(Dmitri Baltermants), 43(George Rodger), 44(Anatoli Garanin), 45(Georgi Zelma), 54-55(Robert Capa), 56(Robert Capa), 57(Robert Capa), 60-61(Ye Haldei), 63(Robert Capa), 64-65(Robert Capa), 66(Robert Capa), 68-69(Robert Capa), 72-73(Robert Capa), 76-77(Robert Capa), 89(Robert Capa), 90(Robert Capa), 91(Robert Capa), 92(Robert Capa), 96-97(Ye Haldei), 108(Wayne Miller), 109(Wayne Miller), 111(Ernst Haas).
Lee Miller Archives, 1985, pages: 21, 70, 79, 93, 98, 100, 101.
Novosti Press, pages: 16(Dmitri Baltermants), 28(Max Alpert), 108(Victor Grebnev).
Parade, page: 20(Bela Zola).
TRH, London, page: 59(US Navy/Charles Fenno Jacobs).
UPI/Bettmann Newsphotos, pages: 17, 27.
U.S. Army, page: 49(Robert Capa).
U.S.M.C., page: 19(Louis Lowery).